To renew this book, phone 0845 1202811 or visit
our website at www.libcat.oxfordshire.gov.uk
(for both options you will need your library PIN
number available from your library),
or contact any Oxfordshire library

 OXFORDSHIRE
COUNTY COUNCIL

L017-64 (01/13)

3303448808

Opposites!

BIG
AND
SMALL

BY EMILIE DUFRESNE

©2018
Book Life
King's Lynn
Norfolk PE30 4LS

ISBN: 978-1-78637-416-5

Written by:
Emilie Dufresne

Edited by:
Kirsty Holmes

Designed by:
Jasmine Pointer

A catalogue record for this book
is available from the British Library.

CONTENTS

Page 4   What Are Opposites?

Page 6   Land Mammals

Page 8   Rocks

Page 10   Planets

Page 12   Fruit

Page 14   Sea Creatures

Page 16   Cities

Page 18   Dinosaurs

Page 20   Activity

Page 22   Answers

Page 24   Glossary and Index

Words that look like **this** can be found in the glossary on page 24.

WHAT ARE OPPOSITES?

An opposite is when two things are completely different.

SOME EXAMPLES OF OPPOSITES ARE...

LIGHT AND DARK

HARD AND SOFT

WET AND DRY

LOUD AND quiet

HOT AND COLD

BIG AND small

Something that is **BIG** is not the same as something that is small.

BIG
AND
small
ARE
OPPOSITES.

LAND MAMMALS

Mammals are warm-blooded animals. They make milk to feed their babies.

THE AFRICAN ELEPHANT IS THE BIGGEST LAND MAMMAL.

THE AFRICAN ELEPHANT AND THE BUMBLEBEE BAT ARE OPPOSITES!

The bumblebee bat is one of the smallest land mammals.

ROCKS

Mount Augustus is one of the biggest rocks on Earth. It is in the Australian **outback**.

Pebbles are rocks that have been worn down by the weather. Pebbles are small.

MOUNT AUGUSTUS AND PEBBLES ARE OPPOSITES!

PLANETS

Jupiter is the biggest planet in our solar system.

EARTH

JUPITER

JUPITER IS AROUND 11 TIMES LARGER THAN EARTH!

MERCURY

JUPITER AND MERCURY ARE OPPOSITES!

EARTH

Mercury is the smallest planet in our solar system.

FRUIT

Watermelons are a big fruit. They are green on the outside and pink in the middle.

THE AVERAGE WATERMELON WEIGHS OVER 5 KILOGRAMS.

ONE BLUEBERRY ONLY WEIGHS AROUND ONE GRAM!

WATERMELONS AND BLUEBERRIES ARE OPPOSITES.

Blueberries are a small fruit. They are blue on the outside and green in the middle.

SEA CREATURES

The blue whale is the biggest creature in the sea.
It can grow up to 35 metres.

MAXIMUM HEIGHT: 2.4 CENTIMETRES!

BLUE WHALES AND PYGMY SEAHORSES ARE OPPOSITES.

The pygmy seahorse is one of the smallest creatures in the sea.

CITIES

Tokyo has one of the biggest **populations** in the world.

AROUND 35 MILLION PEOPLE LIVE IN TOKYO!

TOKYO AND VATICAN CITY ARE OPPOSITES.

Vatican City is a small city. It has a population of around 800 people.

DINOSAURS

Scientists believe that Titanosaur was one of the biggest dinosaurs.

SCIENTISTS THINK THEY WEIGHED AROUND 70 TONS. THAT'S AROUND 15 MALE ELEPHANTS!

Microraptor is thought to be one of the smallest land dinosaurs.

AROUND ONE METRE

TITANOSAUR AND MICRORAPTOR ARE OPPOSITES.

ACTIVITY

Which of these things are **BIG**, and which are small?

BUMBLEBEE BAT

TITANOSAUR

WATERMELON

AFRICAN ELEPHANT

BLUEBERRIES

MICRORAPTOR

ANSWERS

AFRICAN ELEPHANT

WATERLEMON

TITANOSAUR

That's right! These ones are **BIG**!

These ones are small !

BUMBLEBEE BAT

BLUEBERRIES

MICRORAPTOR

GLOSSARY

maximum   the biggest amount possible or allowed

outback   a rural area found in Australia and New Zealand where few people live

populations   the number of people living in a place

INDEX

animals 6–7, 14–15, 18–19

food 12–13

outback 8

population 16–17

Photocredits:

Images are courtesy of Shutterstock.com. With thanks to Getty Images, Thinkstock Photo and iStockphoto.
Front cover - asharkyu, Thasneem, donatas1205, topseller, Lightspring, Martin Gallie, Naom Armonn, Ortis, Brian Kinney, Marc Bruxelle, Luciano Mortula - LGM, All for you friend, Sebastian Knight, andrea crisante, MichaelJayBerlin, Tim UR, Victeah, Carlos Caetano, Computer Earth. 2 – pattang. 3 - Lightspring, asharkyu. 4 – sashahaltam. 5 - Eric Isslee. 6 – Donovan van Staden. 7 - Dave Montreuil. 8 - Chris Hart 77. 9 – Rebecca Lambertsen. 10 – Tristan3D. 11 – Dotted Yeti. 12 – Andrii Zastrozhnov. 13 – Andris Tkacenko. 14 – Atomic Roderick. 15 – Fiona Ayerst. 16 – aon168. 17 – Adrian Flory. 18 – Kostyantyn Ivanyshen. 19 – Warpaint, sumroeng chinnapan. 20 - Dave Montreuil, Kostyantyn Ivanyshen, Andrii Zastrozhnov. 21 - Donovan van Staden, Andris Tkacenko, Warpaint. 22 -Donovan van Staden, Andrii Zastrozhnov, Kostyantyn Ivanyshen. 23 - Dave Montreuil, Andris Tkacenko, Warpaint. 24 - Victeah.